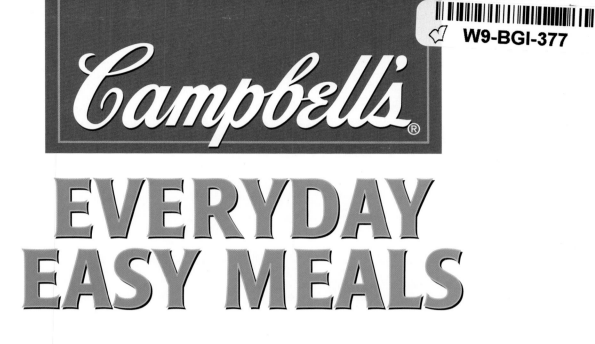

Campbell's

EVERYDAY EASY MEALS

For more delicious recipes and easy meal ideas, visit the
Campbell's Web site at **www.campbellsoup.com**

Homemade in 20 Minutes

Prep/Cook Time: 20 minutes *20 minutes or less!*

½ package *uncooked* linguine (8 ounces)
1 cup fresh *or* frozen broccoli flowerets
2 tablespoons butter *or* margarine
1 pound skinless, boneless chicken breasts, cubed
1 can (10¾ ounces) CAMPBELL'S Condensed Cream of Mushroom Soup *or* 98% Fat Free Cream of Mushroom Soup
½ cup milk
½ cup grated Parmesan cheese
¼ teaspoon freshly ground pepper

1 Prepare linguine according to package directions. Add broccoli for last 4 minutes of cooking time.

2 In medium skillet over medium-high heat, heat butter. Add chicken and cook until browned, stirring often. Drain.

3 Add soup, milk, cheese, pepper and linguine mixture and cook through, stirring occasionally. Serve with additional Parmesan cheese.

Serves 4

Chicken & Broccoli Alfredo

15-MINUTE CHICKEN & RICE DINNER

Prep/Cook Time: 15 minutes *20 minutes or less!*

> 1 tablespoon vegetable oil
> 4 skinless, boneless chicken breast halves (about 1 pound)
> 1 can (10¾ ounces) CAMPBELL'S Condensed Cream of Chicken Soup *or* 98% Fat Free Cream of Chicken Soup
> 1½ cups water*
> ¼ teaspoon paprika
> ¼ teaspoon pepper
> 2 cups fresh *or* thawed frozen broccoli flowerets
> 1½ cups *uncooked* Minute® Original Rice

1 In medium skillet over medium-high heat, heat oil. Add chicken and cook 8 minutes or until browned. Set chicken aside. Pour off fat.

2 Add soup, water, paprika and pepper. Heat to a boil.

3 Stir in broccoli and rice . Place chicken on rice mixture. Season chicken with additional paprika and pepper. Reduce heat to low. Cover and cook 5 minutes or until chicken is no longer pink.   *Serves 4*

*For creamier rice, increase water to 1⅔ cups.

15-Minute Chicken & Rice Dinner

15-MINUTE HERBED CHICKEN

20 minutes or less!

1 tablespoon vegetable oil
4 skinless, boneless chicken breast halves (about
   1 pound)
1 can (10¾ ounces) CAMPBELL'S Condensed Cream of
   Chicken with Herbs Soup
½ cup milk
   Broth Simmered Rice*

1 In medium skillet over medium-high heat, heat oil. Add chicken and cook 8 minutes or until browned. Set chicken aside. Pour off fat.

2 Add soup and milk. Heat to a boil. Return chicken to pan. Reduce heat to low. Cover and cook 5 minutes or until chicken is no longer pink.   *Serves 4*

*Broth Simmered Rice: In medium saucepan over medium-high heat, heat 1 can CAMPBELL'S Condensed Chicken Broth and 1 cup water to a boil. Stir in 2 cups *uncooked* Minute® Original Rice. Cover and remove from heat. Let stand 5 minutes. Fluff with fork.

Creamy Mushroom-Garlic Chicken: Substitute 1 can (10¾ ounces) CAMPBELL'S Condensed Cream of Mushroom with Roasted Garlic Soup for Cream of Chicken with Herbs Soup.

Quick Herbed Chicken Dijon: In step 2 add 1 tablespoon Dijon-style mustard with the soup and milk.

Top to bottom: Hearty Chicken Noodle Soup (page 15), Broth Simmered Rice and 15-Minute Herbed Chicken

SPEEDY CHICKEN ENCHILADAS

Prep/Cook Time: 20 minutes   *20 minutes or less!*

1 pound skinless, boneless chicken breasts, cubed
1 can (10¾ ounces) CAMPBELL'S Condensed Cream of Chicken Soup *or* 98% Fat Free Cream of Chicken Soup
1 cup PACE Thick & Chunky Salsa *or* Picante Sauce
8 flour tortillas (6-inch)
1 can (10¾ ounces) CAMPBELL'S Condensed Cheddar Cheese Soup

1. In medium nonstick skillet over medium-high heat, cook chicken until browned and juices evaporate, stirring often. Add chicken soup and ½ *cup* salsa. Heat to a boil, stirring occasionally.

2. Along one side of each tortilla, spread about ⅓ *cup* chicken mixture. Roll up each tortilla around filling and place seam-side down in 2-quart microwave-safe baking dish.

3. Mix cheese soup and remaining salsa and pour over enchiladas.

4. Cover and microwave on HIGH 5 minutes or until hot.

Serves 4

Tip   *Warm tortillas for easier handling. Stack tortillas and wrap in damp, microwave-safe paper towels. Microwave on HIGH for 15 seconds for 2 tortillas; add 15 seconds to time for every 2 additional tortillas.*

Top to bottom: Speedy Chicken Enchiladas and Beef & Cheddar Soft Tacos (page 14)

BEEF & CHEDDAR SOFT TACOS

(photo on page 13)

Prep/Cook Time: 15 minutes   *20 minutes or less!*

> **1 pound ground beef**
> **1 can (10¾ ounces) CAMPBELL'S Condensed Cheddar Cheese Soup**
> **½ cup PACE Thick & Chunky Salsa *or* Picante Sauce**
> **8 flour tortillas (8-inch)**
> **2 cups shredded lettuce (about ½ small head)**

1 In medium skillet over medium-high heat, cook beef until browned, stirring to separate meat. Pour off fat.

2 Add soup and salsa. Reduce heat to low and heat through.

3 Spoon *about ⅓ cup* meat mixture down center of each tortilla. Top with lettuce. Fold tortilla around filling. Serve with additional salsa.

Serves 4

SAUCY PORK CHOPS

(photo on page 17)

Prep/Cook Time: 15 minutes   *20 minutes or less!*

> **1 tablespoon vegetable oil**
> **4 pork chops, ½ inch thick (about 1 pound)**
> **1 can (10¾ ounces) CAMPBELL'S Condensed Cream of Onion Soup**
> **¼ cup water**

1 In medium skillet over medium-high heat, heat oil. Add chops and cook 8 minutes or until browned. Set chops aside. Pour off fat.

2 Add soup and water. Heat to a boil. Return chops to pan. Reduce heat to low. Cover and cook 5 minutes or until chops are no longer pink.

Serves 4

HEARTY CHICKEN NOODLE SOUP

(photo on page 11)

Prep/Cook Time: 20 minutes   *20 minutes or less!*

- **2 cans (10½ ounces *each*) CAMPBELL'S Condensed Chicken Broth**
- **1 cup water**
- **Generous dash pepper**
- **2 skinless, boneless chicken breast halves, cut up**
- **1 medium carrot, sliced (about ½ cup)**
- **1 stalk celery, sliced (about ½ cup)**
- **½ cup *uncooked* medium egg noodles**

1 In medium saucepan mix broth, water, pepper, chicken, carrot and celery. Over medium-high heat, heat to a boil.

2 Stir in noodles. Reduce heat to medium. Cook 10 minutes or until noodles are done, stirring often.   *Serves 4*

Tip   *Save time by using precut carrots and celery from your supermarket salad bar.*

SEAFOOD TOMATO ALFREDO

Prep/Cook Time: 20 minutes   *20 minutes or less!*

1 tablespoon margarine *or* butter
1 medium onion, chopped (about ½ cup)
1 can (10¾ ounces) CAMPBELL'S Condensed Cream of
    Mushroom with Roasted Garlic Soup
½ cup milk
1 cup diced canned tomatoes
1 pound firm white fish (cod, haddock *or* halibut), cut
    into 2-inch pieces
4 cups hot cooked linguine (about 8 ounces uncooked)

1 In medium skillet over medium-high heat, heat margarine. Add onion and cook until tender.

2 Add soup, milk and tomatoes. Heat to a boil. Add fish. Reduce heat to low. Cook 10 minutes or until fish flakes easily when tested with a fork. Serve over linguine.   *Serves 4*

Tip

Salted water takes longer to boil. To save time, don't salt water until after it is boiling.

**Top to bottom: Saucy Pork Chop (page 14) and
Seafood Tomato Alfredo**

ASPARAGUS & HAM POTATO TOPPER

Prep/Cook Time: 10 minutes *20 minutes or less!*

    4 hot baked potatoes, split
    1 cup diced cooked ham
    1 can (10¾ ounces) CAMPBELL'S Condensed Cream of
        Asparagus Soup
    Shredded Cheddar *or* Swiss cheese (optional)

1 Place hot baked potatoes on microwave-safe plate. Carefully fluff up potatoes with fork.

2 Top each potato with ham. Stir soup in can until smooth. Spoon soup over potatoes. Top with cheese, if desired. Microwave on HIGH 4 minutes or until hot.   *Serves 4*

LEMON ASPARAGUS CHICKEN

Prep/Cook Time: 20 minutes *20 minutes or less!*

    1 tablespoon vegetable oil
    4 skinless, boneless chicken breast halves (about
        1 pound)
    1 can (10¾ ounces) CAMPBELL'S Condensed Cream of
        Asparagus Soup
    ¼ cup milk
    1 tablespoon lemon juice
    ⅛ teaspoon pepper

1 In medium skillet over medium-high heat, heat oil. Add chicken and cook 8 minutes or until browned. Set chicken aside. Pour off fat.

2 Add soup, milk, lemon juice and pepper. Heat to a boil. Return chicken to pan. Reduce heat to low. Cover and cook 5 minutes or until chicken is no longer pink.   *Serves 4*

**Top to bottom: Asparagus & Ham Potato Topper and
Lemon Asparagus Chicken**

EASY SKILLET BEEF & HASH BROWNS

Prep/Cook Time: 20 minutes   *20 minutes or less!*

     1 pound ground beef
     1 can (10¾ ounces) CAMPBELL'S Condensed Cream of
          Celery Soup *or* 98% Fat Free Cream of Celery Soup
     ½ cup water
     ¼ cup ketchup
     1 tablespoon Worcestershire sauce
     2 cups frozen diced potatoes (hash browns)
     3 slices process American cheese (about 3 ounces)

1 In medium skillet over medium-high heat, cook beef until browned, stirring to separate meat. Pour off fat.

2 Add soup, water, ketchup and Worcestershire. Heat to a boil. Stir in potatoes. Reduce heat to medium-low. Cover and cook 10 minutes or until potatoes are done, stirring occasionally. Top with cheese.   *Serves 4*

Top to bottom: Quick Beef Skillet (page 22) and Easy Skillet Beef & Hash Browns

QUICK BEEF SKILLET

(photo on page 21)

Prep/Cook Time: 15 minutes   *20 minutes or less!*

> 1 pound ground beef
> 1 can (10¾ ounces) CAMPBELL'S Condensed Tomato
>   Soup
> ¼ cup water
> 1 tablespoon Worcestershire sauce
> ¼ teaspoon pepper
> 1 can (about 15 ounces) sliced potatoes, drained
> 1 can (about 8 ounces) sliced carrots, drained

1 In medium skillet over medium-high heat, cook beef until browned, stirring to separate meat. Pour off fat.

2 Add soup, water, Worcestershire, pepper, potatoes and carrots. Reduce heat to low and heat through.   *Serves 4*

> *Tip*   *Store ground meat in the coldest part of the refrigerator (35°F.) for no longer than 2 days.*

ITALIAN BURGER MELT

(photo on page 25)

Prep/Cook Time: 20 minutes　　*20 minutes or less!*

> **1 pound ground beef**
> **1 can (11⅛ ounces) CAMPBELL'S Condensed Italian Tomato Soup**
> **¼ cup water**
> **4 slices mozzarella, process American *or* Monterey Jack cheese (about 4 ounces)**
> **4 hamburger rolls, split and toasted**

1 Shape beef into 4 patties, ½ inch thick.

2 In medium skillet over medium-high heat, cook patties until browned. Set patties aside. Pour off fat.

3 Add soup and water. Heat to a boil. Return patties to pan. Reduce heat to low. Cover and cook 10 minutes or until patties are no longer pink (160°F.).

4 Place cheese on patties and cook until cheese is melted. Place patties on 4 roll halves. Top with soup mixture and remaining roll halves. 　　*Makes 4 sandwiches*

Serving Idea: Serve with **Swanson Simple Seasoned Pasta.** In medium saucepan over medium-high heat, heat to a boil 2 cans (14½ ounces **each**) SWANSON Seasoned Chicken Broth with Italian Herbs. Stir in 3 cups **uncooked** corkscrew pasta. Reduce heat to medium. Simmer gently 10 minutes or until pasta is done, stirring occasionally. Serves about 6.

FRENCH ONION BURGERS

20 minutes or less!

1 pound ground beef
1 can (10½ ounces) CAMPBELL'S Condensed French
    Onion Soup
4 round hard rolls, split
4 slices cheese (use your favorite)

1 Shape beef into 4 patties, ½ inch thick.

2 In medium skillet over medium-high heat, cook patties until browned. Set patties aside. Pour off fat.

3 Add soup. Heat to a boil. Return patties to pan. Reduce heat to low. Cover and cook 10 minutes or until patties are no longer pink (160°F.).

4 Place cheese on patties and cook until cheese is melted. Place patties on 4 roll halves. Serve with soup mixture for dipping.

Makes 4 sandwiches

**Top to bottom: Italian Burger Melt (page 23) and
French Onion Burger**

Campbell's®

Speedy Skillets

COUNTRY SKILLET SUPPER

Prep Time: 5 minutes   **Cook Time:** 25 minutes

    1 pound ground beef
    1 medium onion, chopped (about ½ cup)
    ⅛ teaspoon garlic powder *or* 1 clove garlic, minced
    1 can (10¾ ounces) CAMPBELL'S Condensed Golden
        Mushroom Soup
    1 can (10½ ounces) CAMPBELL'S Condensed Beef Broth
    1 can (14½ ounces) diced tomatoes
    1 small zucchini, sliced (about 1 cup)
    ½ teaspoon dried thyme leaves, crushed
    1½ cups *uncooked* corkscrew pasta

1 In medium skillet over medium-high heat, cook beef, onion and garlic powder until beef is browned, stirring to separate meat. Pour off fat.

2 Add soup, broth, tomatoes, zucchini and thyme. Heat to a boil. Stir in pasta. Reduce heat to low. Cook 15 minutes or until pasta is done, stirring often.   *Serves 4*

Country Skillet Supper Provençal: Top with sliced pitted ripe olives.

Country Skillet Supper

JAMBALAYA ONE DISH

Prep Time: 10 minutes   **Cook Time:** 20 minutes

    1 tablespoon vegetable oil
    ½ pound skinless, boneless chicken breasts, cut up
    ½ pound hot Italian pork sausage, sliced
    ¼ teaspoon garlic powder *or* 2 cloves garlic, minced
    1 can (10½ ounces) CAMPBELL'S Condensed French
       Onion Soup
    ⅓ cup PACE Picante Sauce *or* Thick & Chunky Salsa
    1 cup *uncooked* Minute® Original Rice
    ½ cup frozen peas
    ½ pound frozen cooked large shrimp

1 In medium skillet over medium-high heat, heat oil. Add chicken, sausage and garlic powder and cook 5 minutes or until browned, stirring often. Pour off fat.

2 Add soup and picante sauce. Heat to a boil. Stir in rice, peas and shrimp. Reduce heat to low. Cover and cook 5 minutes or until chicken and sausage are no longer pink and most of liquid is absorbed.

Serves 4

Jambalaya One Dish

EASY BEEF & PASTA

20 minutes or less!

> 1 **pound boneless beef sirloin steak, ¾ inch thick**
> 1 **tablespoon vegetable oil**
> 1 **can (10¾ ounces) CAMPBELL'S Condensed Tomato
>   Soup**
> ½ **cup water**
> 1 **bag (about 16 ounces) frozen side dish seasoned pasta
>   and vegetable combination**

1 Slice beef into very thin strips.

2 In medium skillet over medium-high heat, heat oil. Add beef and cook until beef is browned and juices evaporate, stirring often.

3 Add soup, water and vegetable combination. Heat to a boil. Reduce heat to low. Cover and cook 5 minutes or until beef and vegetables are done, stirring occasionally. *Serves 4*

For easier slicing, place beef in the freezer for 45 to 60 minutes or until it is partially frozen, then cut it into very thin slices.

**Top to bottom: Chili Chicken Pasta Topper (page 37)
and Easy Beef & Pasta**

COUNTRY HERBED CHICKEN & VEGETABLES

Prep Time: 5 minutes   **Cook Time:** 25 minutes

> 1 tablespoon vegetable oil
> 1 pound skinless, boneless chicken breasts, cut up
> 1 can (10¾ ounces) CAMPBELL'S Condensed Cream of Chicken with Herbs Soup
> ½ cup milk
> 1 bag (16 ounces) frozen vegetable combination (broccoli, cauliflower, carrots)

1 In medium skillet over medium-high heat, heat oil. Add chicken and cook until browned, stirring often. Set chicken aside. Pour off fat.

2 Add soup, milk and vegetables. Heat to a boil. Return chicken to pan. Reduce heat to low. Cover and cook 10 minutes or until vegetables are tender. *Serves 4*

Tip *Substitute your favorite frozen vegetable combination for the broccoli, cauliflower and carrots combo called for here.*

Top to bottom: Herb Roasted Chicken & Potatoes (page 69) and Country Herbed Chicken & Vegetables

SHORTCUT STROGANOFF

Prep Time: 5 minutes   **Cook Time:** 30 minutes

- 1 pound boneless beef sirloin steak, ¾ inch thick
- 1 tablespoon vegetable oil
- 1 can (10¾ ounces) CAMPBELL'S Condensed Cream of Mushroom Soup *or* 98% Fat Free Cream of Mushroom Soup
- 1 can (10½ ounces) CAMPBELL'S Condensed Beef Broth
- 1 cup water
- 2 teaspoons Worcestershire sauce
- 3 cups *uncooked* corkscrew pasta
- ½ cup sour cream

1 Slice beef into very thin strips.

2 In medium skillet over medium-high heat, heat oil. Add beef and cook until beef is browned and juices evaporate, stirring often.

3 Add soup, broth, water and Worcestershire. Heat to a boil. Stir in pasta. Reduce heat to medium. Cook 15 minutes or until pasta is done, stirring often. Stir in sour cream. Heat through.

Serves 4

Top to bottom: Beef & Broccoli (page 36) and Shortcut Stroganoff

BEEF & BROCCOLI

(photo on page 35)

Prep/Cook Time: 25 minutes

> **1 pound boneless beef sirloin *or* top round steak, ¾ inch thick**
> **1 tablespoon vegetable oil**
> **1 can (10¾ ounces) CAMPBELL'S Condensed Tomato Soup**
> **3 tablespoons soy sauce**
> **1 tablespoon vinegar**
> **1 teaspoon garlic powder**
> **¼ teaspoon crushed red pepper (optional)**
> **3 cups fresh *or* thawed frozen broccoli flowerets**
> **4 cups hot cooked rice**

1 Slice beef into very thin strips.

2 In medium skillet over medium-high heat, heat oil. Add beef and stir-fry until browned and juices evaporate.

3 Add soup, soy sauce, vinegar, garlic powder and pepper. Heat to a boil. Reduce heat to medium. Add broccoli and cook until tender-crisp, stirring occasionally. Serve over rice.   *Serves 4*

Tip To thaw broccoli, microwave on HIGH 3 minutes.

CHILI CHICKEN PASTA TOPPER

(photo on page 31)

Prep/Cook Time: 20 minutes   *20 minutes or less!*

- 1 tablespoon vegetable oil
- 1 pound skinless, boneless chicken breasts, cubed
- 1 can (10¾ ounces) CAMPBELL'S Condensed Cream of Chicken with Herbs Soup
- ½ cup milk
- 2 tablespoons grated Parmesan cheese
- 1 teaspoon chili powder
- ½ teaspoon garlic powder
- 4 cups hot cooked corkscrew pasta (about 3 cups uncooked)

1 In medium skillet over medium-high heat, heat oil. Add chicken and cook until browned, stirring often.

2 Add soup, milk, cheese, chili powder and garlic powder and cook through, stirring often. Serve over pasta.   *Serves* 4

When a recipe will be served over pasta or rice, save time by heating the cooking water while you're preparing the recipe. It'll be ready when you are!

Campbell's®

Restaurant Style at Home

ASIAN CHICKEN STIR-FRY

20 minutes or less!

- 1 tablespoon vegetable oil
- 1 pound skinless, boneless chicken breasts, cut into strips
- 1 can (10¾ ounces) CAMPBELL'S Condensed Golden Mushroom Soup
- 3 tablespoons soy sauce
- 1 teaspoon garlic powder
- 1 bag (16 ounces) any frozen vegetable combination, thawed
- 4 cups hot cooked rice

1 In medium skillet over medium-high heat, heat oil. Add chicken and stir-fry until browned and juices evaporate.

2 Add soup, soy sauce and garlic powder. Heat to a boil. Reduce heat to medium. Add vegetables and cook until vegetables are tender-crisp, stirring often. Serve over rice. *Serves 4*

Asian Chicken Stir-Fry

CHICKEN QUESADILLAS & FIESTA RICE

Prep/Cook Time: 20 minutes   *20 minutes or less!*

1 pound skinless, boneless chicken breasts, cubed
1 can (10¾ ounces) CAMPBELL'S Condensed Cheddar
    Cheese Soup
½ cup PACE Thick & Chunky Salsa *or* Picante Sauce
    (Medium)
10 flour tortillas (8-inch)
    Fiesta Rice*

1 Preheat oven to 425°F.

2 In medium nonstick skillet over medium-high heat, cook chicken
5 minutes or until no longer pink and juices evaporate, stirring
often. Add soup and salsa. Heat to a boil, stirring occasionally.

3 Place tortillas on 2 baking sheets. Top **half** of each tortilla with
about ⅓ cup soup mixture. Spread to within ½ inch of edge.
Moisten edges of tortilla with water. Fold over and press edges
together.

4 Bake 5 minutes or until hot.   *Serves 4*

*Fiesta Rice: In saucepan heat 1 can CAMPBELL'S Condensed
Chicken Broth, ½ cup water and ½ cup PACE Thick & Chunky
Salsa *or* Picante Sauce to a boil. Stir in 2 cups *uncooked*
Minute® Original Rice. Cover and remove from heat. Let stand
5 minutes.

Chicken Quesadillas & Fiesta Rice

PAN ROASTED
VEGETABLE & CHICKEN PIZZA

Prep Time: 20 minutes   **Cook Time:** 12 minutes

Vegetable cooking spray
¾ pound skinless, boneless chicken breasts, cubed
3 cups cut-up vegetables*
⅛ teaspoon garlic powder *or* 1 clove garlic, minced
1 can (10¾ ounces) CAMPBELL'S Condensed Cream of
     Mushroom Soup *or* 98% Fat Free Cream of
     Mushroom Soup
1 Italian bread shell (12-inch)
1 cup shredded Monterey Jack cheese (4 ounces)

1 Spray medium skillet with vegetable cooking spray and heat over medium-high heat 1 minute. Add chicken and cook 10 minutes or until browned, stirring often. Set chicken aside.

2 Remove pan from heat. Spray with cooking spray. Reduce heat to medium. Add vegetables and garlic powder. Cook until tender-crisp. Add soup. Return chicken to pan. Heat through.

3 Spread chicken mixture over shell to within ¼ inch of edge. Top with cheese. Bake at 450°F. for 12 minutes or until cheese is melted.

Serves 4

*Use a combination of sliced zucchini, red *or* green pepper cut into 2-inch long strips, and thinly sliced onion.

Top to bottom: Creamy Chicken Risotto (page 44) and Pan Roasted Vegetable & Chicken Pizza

CREAMY CHICKEN RISOTTO

(photo on page 43)

Prep Time: 10 minutes   **Cook Time:** 35 minutes

1 tablespoon vegetable oil
1 pound skinless, boneless chicken breasts, cut up
1 can (10¾ ounces) CAMPBELL'S Condensed Cream of Mushroom with Roasted Garlic Soup
1 can (10½ ounces) CAMPBELL'S Condensed Chicken Broth
¾ cup water
1 small carrot, shredded (about ⅓ cup)
2 medium green onions, sliced (about ¼ cup)
1 tablespoon grated Parmesan cheese
1 cup *uncooked* regular long-grain white rice

1 In medium skillet over medium-high heat, heat oil. Add chicken and cook until browned, stirring often.

2 Add soup, broth, water, carrot, onions and cheese. Heat to a boil. Stir in rice. Reduce heat to low. Cover and cook 25 minutes until chicken and rice are done and most of liquid is absorbed, stirring occasionally.

Serves 4

ORANGE BEEF

(photo on page 47)

Prep Time: 10 minutes   **Cook Time:** 20 minutes

- 1 pound boneless beef sirloin steak, ¾ inch thick
- 2 tablespoons vegetable oil
- 1 medium green pepper, cut into 2-inch long strips (about 1½ cups)
- 1 medium onion, sliced (about ½ cup)
- 1 can (10¾ ounces) CAMPBELL'S Condensed Tomato Soup
- ¼ cup orange juice
- 2 tablespoons soy sauce
- 1 tablespoon vinegar
- 1 teaspoon garlic powder
- 4 cups hot cooked rice

1 Slice beef into very thin strips.

2 In medium skillet over medium-high heat, heat **half** the oil. Add beef and stir-fry until beef is browned and juices evaporate.

3 Reduce heat to medium. Add remaining oil. Add pepper and onion and cook until tender-crisp.

4 Add soup, orange juice, soy sauce, vinegar and garlic powder. Heat through, stirring occasionally. Serve over rice.   *Serves 4*

EASY BEEF TERIYAKI

Prep Time: 10 minutes   **Cook Time:** 20 minutes

- 1 pound boneless beef sirloin steak, ¾ inch thick
- 1 tablespoon vegetable oil
- 1 can (10¾ ounces) CAMPBELL'S Condensed Golden Mushroom Soup
- 2 tablespoons soy sauce
- 1 tablespoon packed brown sugar
- 1 bag (about 16 ounces) frozen Oriental stir-fry vegetables
- 4 cups hot cooked rice

1 Slice beef into very thin strips.

2 In medium skillet over medium-high heat, heat oil. Add beef and stir-fry until beef is browned and juices evaporate.

3 Add soup, soy sauce and sugar. Heat to a boil. Reduce heat to medium. Add vegetables. Cover and cook 5 minutes until vegetables are tender-crisp, stirring occasionally. Serve over rice.

Serves 4

Tip *If a recipe calls for cooked rice, substitute instant rice for regular long grain. It cooks 15 minutes faster.*

Top to bottom: Orange Beef (page 45) and Easy Beef Teriyaki

CHEESESTEAK POCKETS

Prep/Cook Time: 15 minutes   *20 minutes or less!*

1 tablespoon vegetable oil

1 medium onion, sliced (about ½ cup)

1 package (14 ounces) frozen beef *or* chicken sandwich
   steaks, cut into 8 pieces

1 can (10¾ ounces) CAMPBELL'S Condensed Cheddar
   Cheese Soup

1 jar (about 4½ ounces) sliced mushrooms, drained

4 pita breads (6-inch), cut in half, forming two pockets
   each

1 In medium skillet over medium-high heat, heat oil. Add onion
and cook until tender. Add sandwich steaks and cook 5 minutes
or until browned, stirring often. Pour off fat.

2 Add soup and mushrooms. Heat to a boil. Reduce heat to low
and heat through. Spoon meat mixture into pita halves.

Makes 4 sandwiches

**Top to bottom: Buffalo-Style Burger (page 50)
and Cheesesteak Pockets**

BUFFALO–STYLE BURGERS

(photo on page 49)

Prep/Cook Time: 20 minutes   *20 minutes or less!*

  1 **pound ground beef**
  1 **can (10¾ ounces) CAMPBELL'S Condensed Tomato**
     Soup
  ⅛ **teaspoon hot pepper sauce**
  4 **hamburger rolls, split and toasted**
  ½ **cup crumbled blue cheese (about 4 ounces)**

1 Shape beef into 4 patties, ½ inch thick.

2 In medium skillet over medium-high heat, cook patties until browned. Set patties aside. Pour off fat.

3 Add soup and hot pepper sauce. Heat to a boil. Return patties to pan. Reduce heat to low. Cover and cook 10 minutes or until patties are no longer pink (160°F.).

4 Place patties on 4 roll halves. Top with cheese and remaining roll halves.   *Makes 4 sandwiches*

MONTEREY CHICKEN FAJITAS

(photo on page 53)

Prep Time: 10 minutes   **Cook Time:** 20 minutes

> 2 tablespoons vegetable oil
> 1 pound skinless, boneless chicken breasts, cut into strips
> 1 medium green pepper, cut into 2-inch long strips (about 1½ cups)
> 1 medium onion, sliced (about ½ cup)
> 1 can (10¾ ounces) CAMPBELL'S Condensed Cream of Mushroom Soup *or* 98% Fat Free Cream of Mushroom Soup
> ½ cup PACE Thick & Chunky Salsa *or* Picante Sauce
> 8 flour tortillas (8-inch)
> 1 cup shredded Monterey Jack cheese (4 ounces)

1 In medium skillet over medium-high heat, heat *half* the oil. Add chicken and cook until browned and juices evaporate, stirring often. Set chicken aside.

2 Reduce heat to medium. Add remaining oil. Add pepper and onion and cook until tender-crisp. Pour off fat.

3 Add soup and salsa. Heat to a boil. Return chicken to pan and heat through. Spoon *about ½ cup* chicken mixture down center of each tortilla. Top with cheese and additional salsa. Fold tortilla around filling.   *Serves 4*

SOUTHWESTERN CHICKEN & PEPPER WRAPS

Prep Time: 10 minutes   **Cook/Stand Time:** 25 minutes

2 tablespoons vegetable oil
1 pound skinless, boneless chicken breasts, cut into strips
1 medium red pepper, cut into 2-inch long strips (about 1½ cups)
1 medium green pepper, cut into 2-inch long strips (about 1½ cups)
1 small onion, sliced (about ¼ cup)
1 can (10¾ ounces) CAMPBELL'S Condensed Golden Mushroom Soup
1 cup water
1 cup black beans, rinsed and drained (optional)
1 cup *uncooked* Minute® Original Rice
8 flour tortillas (8-inch)

1 In medium skillet over medium-high heat, heat *half* the oil. Add chicken and cook 10 minutes or until no longer pink and juices evaporate, stirring often.

2 Reduce heat to medium. Add remaining oil. Add peppers and onion and cook until tender-crisp, stirring often.

3 Add soup, water and beans. Heat to a boil. Stir in rice. Cover and remove from heat. Let stand 5 minutes.

4 Spoon ¾ *cup* chicken mixture down center of each tortilla. Fold tortilla around filling.   *Serves 4*

Top to bottom: Monterey Chicken Fajita (page 51) and Southwestern Chicken & Pepper Wrap

Quick-Fix Oven Wonders

ONE-DISH CHICKEN & RICE BAKE

Prep Time: 5 minutes   **Cook Time:** 45 minutes

> 1 can (10¾ ounces) CAMPBELL'S Condensed Cream of Mushroom Soup *or* 98% Fat Free Cream of Mushroom Soup
> 1 cup water*
> ¾ cup *uncooked* regular white rice
> ¼ teaspoon paprika
> ¼ teaspoon pepper
> 4 skinless, boneless chicken breast halves (about 1 pound)

1 In 2-quart shallow baking dish mix soup, water, rice, paprika and pepper. Place chicken on rice mixture. Sprinkle with additional paprika and pepper. **Cover.**

2 Bake at 375°F. for 45 minutes or until chicken is no longer pink and rice is done.   *Serves 4*

*For creamier rice, increase water to 1⅓ cups.

Top to bottom: One-Dish Chicken & Stuffing Bake (page 61) and One-Dish Chicken & Rice Bake

SIMPLY DELICIOUS MEAT LOAF

Prep Time: 5 minutes   **Cook Time:** 1 hour 5 minutes

1½ **pounds ground beef**
½ **cup Italian-seasoned dry bread crumbs**
1 **egg, beaten**
1 **can (10¾ ounces) CAMPBELL'S Condensed Golden Mushroom Soup**
¼ **cup water**

1 Mix beef, bread crumbs and egg *thoroughly*. In medium baking pan shape *firmly* into 8- by 4-inch loaf.

2 Bake at 350°F. for 30 minutes. Spread ½ *can* soup over top of meat loaf. Bake 30 minutes more or until meat loaf is no longer pink (160°F.).

3 In small saucepan mix *2 tablespoons* drippings, remaining soup and water. Heat through. Serve with meat loaf.   *Serves 6*

Left to right: Parmesan Potatoes (page 83) and Simply Delicious Meat Loaf

FIESTA CHICKEN & RICE BAKE

Prep Time: 5 minutes   **Cook Time:** 45 minutes

> 1 can (10¾ ounces) CAMPBELL'S Condensed Cream of Chicken Soup *or* 98% Fat Free Cream of Chicken Soup
> 1 cup PACE Thick & Chunky Salsa *or* Picante Sauce
> ½ cup water
> 1 cup whole kernel corn
> ¾ cup *uncooked* regular white rice
> 4 skinless, boneless chicken breast halves (about 1 pound)
>   Paprika
> ½ cup shredded Cheddar cheese (2 ounces)

1 In 2-quart shallow baking dish mix soup, salsa, water, corn and rice. Place chicken on rice mixture. Sprinkle paprika over chicken. **Cover.**

2 Bake at 375°F. for 45 minutes or until chicken is no longer pink and rice is done. Sprinkle with cheese.   *Serves 4*

Top to bottom: Asian Chicken & Rice Bake (page 60) and Fiesta Chicken & Rice Bake

ASIAN CHICKEN & RICE BAKE

(photo on page 59)

Prep Time: 5 minutes   **Cook Time:** 45 minutes

¾ cup *uncooked* regular white rice
4 skinless, boneless chicken breast halves (about 1 pound)
1 can (10¾ ounces) CAMPBELL'S Condensed Golden Mushroom Soup
¾ cup water
2 tablespoons soy sauce
2 tablespoons cider vinegar
2 tablespoons honey
1 teaspoon garlic powder
Paprika

1 Spread rice in 2-quart shallow baking dish. Place chicken on rice.

2 Mix soup, water, soy sauce, vinegar, honey and garlic powder. Pour over chicken. Sprinkle with paprika. **Cover.**

3 Bake at 375°F. for 45 minutes or until chicken is no longer pink and rice is done.   *Serves 4*

Sesame Asian Chicken & Rice Bake: Sprinkle with toasted sesame seeds after baking.

ONE–DISH CHICKEN & STUFFING BAKE

(photo on page 55)

Prep Time: 10 minutes   **Cook Time:** 30 minutes

1¼ cups boiling water
4 tablespoons margarine *or* butter, melted
4 cups PEPPERIDGE FARM Herb Seasoned Stuffing
4 to 6 skinless, boneless chicken breast halves (about 1 to 1½ pounds)
Paprika
1 can (10¾ ounces) CAMPBELL'S Condensed Cream of Mushroom Soup *or* 98% Fat Free Cream of Mushroom Soup
⅓ cup milk
1 tablespoon chopped fresh parsley *or* 1 teaspoon dried parsley flakes

1 Mix water and margarine. Add stuffing. Mix lightly.

2 Spoon stuffing across center of 3-quart shallow baking dish, leaving space on both sides for chicken. Arrange chicken on each side of stuffing. Sprinkle paprika over chicken.

3 Mix soup, milk and parsley. Pour over chicken.

4 **Cover.** Bake at 400°F. for 30 minutes or until chicken is no longer pink.

Serves 4 to 6

GARLIC MASHED POTATOES & BEEF BAKE

Prep Time: 10 minutes   **Cook Time:** 20 minutes

- **1 pound ground beef**
- **1 can (10¾ ounces) CAMPBELL'S Condensed Cream of Mushroom with Roasted Garlic Soup**
- **1 tablespoon Worcestershire sauce**
- **1 bag (16 ounces) frozen vegetable combination (broccoli, cauliflower, carrots), thawed**
- **3 cups hot mashed potatoes**

1 In medium skillet over medium-high heat, cook beef until browned, stirring to separate meat. Pour off fat.

2 In 2-quart shallow baking dish mix beef, ½ **can** soup, Worcestershire and vegetables.

3 Stir remaining soup into potatoes. Spoon potato mixture over beef mixture. Bake at 400°F. for 20 minutes or until hot.

Serves 4

Tip To thaw vegetables, microwave on HIGH 3 minutes.

Garlic Mashed Potatoes & Beef Bake

HAM & BROCCOLI
SHORTCUT STROMBOLI

Prep Time: 10 minutes   **Cook Time:** 20 minutes

   1 package (10 ounces) refrigerated pizza dough
   1 can (10¾ ounces) CAMPBELL'S Condensed Cream of
       Celery Soup
   1 cup cooked chopped broccoli
   2 cups cubed cooked ham
   1 cup shredded Cheddar cheese (4 ounces)

1 Preheat oven to 400°F. Unroll dough onto greased baking sheet. Set aside.

2 Mix soup, broccoli and ham. Spread soup mixture down center of dough. Top with cheese. Fold long sides of dough over filling and pinch and seal. Pinch short sides to seal.

3 Bake 20 minutes or until golden brown. Slice and serve.

Serves 4

Roast Beef & Bean Shortcut Stromboli: Substitute 1 can CAMPBELL'S Condensed Cream of Mushroom Soup, 1 cup cut green beans and 2 cups cubed cooked roast beef for Cream of Celery Soup, broccoli and ham.

Chicken & Vegetable Shortcut Stromboli: Substitute 1 can CAMPBELL'S Condensed Cream of Chicken Soup, 1 cup mixed vegetables and 2 cups cubed cooked chicken *or* turkey for Cream of Celery Soup, broccoli and ham.

**Top to bottom: Cod Vera Cruz (page 68)
and Ham & Broccoli Shortcut Stromboli**

E-Z CHICKEN TORTILLA BAKE

Prep Time: 10 minutes **Cook Time:** 30 minutes

> 1 can (10¾ ounces) CAMPBELL'S Condensed Tomato Soup
> 1 cup PACE Thick & Chunky Salsa *or* Picante Sauce
> ½ cup milk
> 2 cups cubed cooked chicken *or* turkey
> 8 corn tortillas (6- *or* 8-inch), cut into 1-inch pieces
> 1 cup shredded Cheddar cheese (4 ounces)

1 In 2-quart shallow baking dish mix soup, salsa, milk, chicken, tortillas and *half* the cheese. **Cover.**

2 Bake at 400°F. for 30 minutes or until hot. Top with remaining cheese.   *Serves 4*

SLOPPY JOE PIZZA

Prep Time: 10 minutes **Cook Time:** 12 minutes

> ¾ pound ground beef
> 1 can (10¾ ounces) CAMPBELL'S Condensed Tomato Soup
> 1 Italian bread shell (12-inch)
> 1½ cups shredded Cheddar cheese (6 ounces)

1 In medium skillet over medium-high heat, cook beef until browned, stirring to separate meat. Pour off fat.

2 Add soup. Heat through. Spread beef mixture over shell to within ¼ inch of edge. Top with cheese. Bake at 450°F. for 12 minutes or until cheese is melted.   *Serves 4*

Top to bottom: E-Z Chicken Tortilla Bake, 3-Cheese Pasta Bake (page 68) and Sloppy Joe Pizza

COD VERA CRUZ

(photo on page 65)

Prep Time: 10 minutes   **Cook Time:** 20 minutes

  1 pound fresh *or* thawed frozen cod *or* haddock fillets
  1 can (10¾ ounces) CAMPBELL'S Condensed Tomato Soup
  1 can (10½ ounces) CAMPBELL'S Condensed Chicken Broth
  ⅓ cup PACE Thick & Chunky Salsa *or* Picante Sauce
  1 tablespoon lime juice
  2 teaspoons chopped fresh cilantro
  1 teaspoon dried oregano leaves, crushed
  ⅛ teaspoon garlic powder *or* 1 clove garlic, minced
  4 cups hot cooked rice

1 Place fish in 2-quart shallow baking dish.

2 Mix soup, broth, salsa, lime juice, cilantro, oregano and garlic powder. Pour over fish. Bake at 400°F. for 20 minutes or until fish flakes easily when tested with a fork. Serve over rice.

Serves 4

3-CHEESE PASTA BAKE

(photo on page 67)

Prep Time: 10 minutes   **Cook Time:** 20 minutes

  1 can (10¾ ounces) CAMPBELL'S Condensed Cream of
      Mushroom Soup *or* 98% Fat Free Cream of
      Mushroom Soup
  1 package (8 ounces) shredded 2-cheese blend (2 cups)
  ⅓ cup grated Parmesan cheese
  1 cup milk
  ¼ teaspoon pepper
  4 cups cooked corkscrew pasta (about 3 cups uncooked)

In 1½-quart casserole mix soup, cheeses, milk and pepper. Stir in pasta. Bake at 400°F. for 20 minutes or until hot.   *Serves 4*

HERB ROASTED CHICKEN & POTATOES

(photo on page 33)

Prep Time: 10 minutes   **Cook Time:** 30 minutes

    1 large plastic oven bag
    4 skinless, boneless chicken breast halves (about
        1 pound)
    8 small red potatoes, cut into quarters (about 1 pound)
    1 can (10¾ ounces) CAMPBELL'S Condensed Cream of
        Chicken with Herbs Soup
    ¼ cup water
    ½ teaspoon garlic powder
      Chopped fresh parsley for garnish

1 Preheat oven to 375°F. Prepare oven bag according to package directions using **1 tablespoon all-purpose flour.** Place chicken and potatoes in oven bag.

2 In a small bowl mix soup, water and garlic powder. Pour into oven bag. Close bag with nylon tie. Cut 6 (½-inch) slits in top of bag.

3 Bake at 375°F. for 30 minutes or until chicken is no longer pink and potatoes are done. Garnish with parsley.   *Serves 4*

> *Tip* *Coating the inside of the oven bag with flour protects it from bursting during baking.*

EASY CHICKEN POT PIE

Prep Time: 5 minutes   **Cook Time:** 30 minutes

1 can (10¾ ounces) CAMPBELL'S Condensed Cream of
    Chicken with Herbs Soup
1 package (about 9 ounces) frozen mixed vegetables,
    thawed
1 cup cubed cooked chicken *or* turkey
½ cup milk
1 egg
1 cup all-purpose baking mix

1 Preheat oven to 400°F. In 9-inch pie plate mix soup, vegetables and chicken.

2 Mix milk, egg and baking mix. Pour over chicken mixture. Bake 30 minutes or until golden brown.   *Serves 4*

No Guilt Chicken Pot Pie: Substitute 1 can CAMPBELL'S Condensed 98% Fat Free Cream of Chicken Soup for Cream of Chicken with Herbs Soup and 1 cup reduced-fat baking mix for all-purpose baking mix.

Tip

For 1 cup cubed cooked chicken: In medium saucepan over medium heat, in 3 to 4 cups simmering water, cook ½ pound skinless, boneless chicken breasts 5 minutes or until chicken is no longer pink (170°F.).

**No Guilt Chicken Pot Pie (variation of
Easy Chicken Pot Pie)**

FLASH ROASTED
CRISPY RANCH CHICKEN

Prep Time: 5 minutes   **Cook Time:** 20 minutes

> 1 can (10¾ ounces) CAMPBELL'S Condensed Cream of
>   Chicken Soup *or* 98% Fat Free Cream of Chicken
>   Soup
> ½ cup milk
> 1 envelope (1 ounce) ranch salad dressing mix
> 4 skinless, boneless chicken breast halves (about
>   1 pound)
> 1½ cups finely crushed tortilla chips
> 2 tablespoons margarine *or* butter, melted

1 In shallow dish mix soup, milk and dressing mix. Reserve **1 cup** for sauce.

2 Dip chicken into soup mixture. Coat with tortilla chips.

3 Place chicken on greased baking sheet. Drizzle with margarine. Bake at 400°F. for 20 minutes or until chicken is no longer pink.

4 In small saucepan over medium heat, heat reserved soup mixture to a boil. Serve with chicken.   *Serves 4*

Left to right: Creamy Vegetable Medley (page 83)
and Flash Roasted Crispy Ranch Chicken

CORNBREAD CHICKEN POT PIE

Prep Time: 10 minutes   **Cook Time:** 30 minutes

> 1 can (10¾ ounces) CAMPBELL'S Condensed Cream of Chicken Soup *or* 98% Fat Free Cream of Chicken Soup
> 1 can (about 8 ounces) whole kernel corn, drained
> 2 cups cubed cooked chicken *or* turkey
> 1 package (8½ ounces) corn muffin mix
> ¾ cup milk
> 1 egg
> ½ cup shredded Cheddar cheese (2 ounces)

1 Preheat oven to 400°F. In 9-inch pie plate mix soup, corn and chicken.

2 Mix muffin mix, milk and egg. Pour over chicken mixture. Bake for 30 minutes or until golden. Sprinkle with cheese.

Serves 4

Cornbread Chicken Chili Pot Pie: In Step 1 add 1 can (about 4 ounces) chopped green chilies, drained, with the corn.

Tip

Don't waste time shredding or grating cheese. Buy packaged shredded/grated cheese at the store. You'll save at least 5 minutes, and you won't have to clean the grater!

Cornbread Chicken Pot Pie

Simple Sides

GREEN BEAN BAKE

Prep Time: 10 minutes   **Cook Time:** 30 minutes

  1 can (10¾ ounces) CAMPBELL'S Condensed Cream of Mushroom Soup *or* 98% Fat Free Cream of Mushroom Soup
½ cup milk
  1 teaspoon soy sauce
    Dash pepper
  4 cups cooked cut green beans*
  1 can (2.8 ounces) French's® French Fried Onions (1⅓ cups)

1 In 1½-quart casserole mix soup, milk, soy sauce, pepper, beans and ½ *can* onions.

2 Bake at 350°F. for 25 minutes or until hot.

3 Stir. Sprinkle remaining onions over bean mixture. Bake 5 minutes more or until onions are golden.   *Serves 6*

*Use 1 bag (16 to 20 ounces) frozen green beans, 2 packages (9 ounces each) frozen green beans, 2 cans (about 16 ounces each) green beans or about 1½ pounds fresh green beans for this recipe.

Green Bean Bake

CHEESY BROCCOLI

Prep/Cook Time: 10 minutes   *20 minutes or less!*

> 1 can (10¾ ounces) **CAMPBELL'S Condensed Cheddar Cheese Soup**
> ¼ **cup milk**
> 4 **cups frozen broccoli cuts**

1 In 2-quart microwave-safe casserole mix soup and milk. Add broccoli.

2 Cover and microwave on HIGH 8 minutes or until broccoli is tender-crisp, stirring once during heating.   *Serves 4*

CHEESE FRIES

Prep/Cook Time: 20 minutes   *20 minutes or less!*

> 1 **bag (32 ounces) frozen French fried potatoes**
> 1 **can (10¾ ounces) CAMPBELL'S Condensed Cheddar Cheese Soup**

1 On baking sheet bake potatoes according to package directions.

2 Push potatoes into pile in center of baking sheet. Stir soup in can and spoon over potatoes.

3 Bake 3 minutes more or until soup is hot.   *Serves 6*

Nacho Cheese Fries: Substitute CAMPBELL'S Condensed Fiesta Nacho Cheese Soup for the Cheddar Cheese Soup.

Top to bottom: Cheese Fries and Cheesy Broccoli

CHEDDARY POUCH POTATOES

Prep Time: 5 minutes   **Cook Time:** 25 minutes

    1 can (10¾ ounces) **CAMPBELL'S Condensed Cheddar Cheese Soup**
    ¼ **cup milk**
    ½ **teaspoon garlic powder**
    ¼ **teaspoon onion powder**
    4 **cups frozen steak fries**
    Paprika

1 In large bowl mix soup, milk, garlic powder and onion powder. Stir in potatoes.

2 Cut four 14-inch squares of heavy-duty aluminum foil. Spoon *1 cup* soup mixture onto each square, arranging potatoes to make a single layer. Sprinkle with paprika. Bring up sides of foil and double fold. Double fold ends to make packet.

3 Place potato packets on grill rack over medium-hot coals. Grill 25 minutes or until potatoes are tender. *Serves 4*

Cheddary Oven Pouch Potatoes: In Step 3, on baking sheet bake packets at 350°F. for 25 minutes.

Top to bottom: Cheddar Broccoli Bake (page 82) and Cheddary Pouch Potatoes

CHEDDAR BROCCOLI BAKE

(photo on page 81)

Prep Time: 10 minutes   **Cook Time:** 30 minutes

    1 can (10¾ ounces) CAMPBELL'S Condensed Cheddar
        Cheese Soup
    ½ cup milk
        Dash pepper
    4 cups cooked broccoli cuts
    1 can (2.8 ounces) French's® French Fried Onions
        (1⅓ cups)

1 In 1½-quart casserole mix soup, milk, pepper, broccoli and
½ **can** onions.

2 Bake at 350°F. for 25 minutes or until hot.

3 Stir. Sprinkle remaining onions over broccoli mixture. Bake 5
minutes more or until onions are golden.   *Serves 6*

Tip *Two pounds of fresh broccoli will yield 4 cups broccoli cuts.*

PARMESAN POTATOES

(photo on page 57)

Prep Time: 5 minutes   **Cook Time:** 45 minutes

    1 can (10¾ ounces) CAMPBELL'S Condensed Cheddar
         Cheese Soup
½ cup milk
½ cup grated Parmesan cheese
¼ teaspoon pepper
    4 medium white potatoes, cut into 1-inch pieces (about
         4 cups)
    1 can (2.8 ounces) French's® French Fried Onions
         (1⅓ cups)

1 In greased shallow 2-quart baking dish mix soup, milk, cheese and pepper. Stir in potatoes and ½ **can** onions.

2 Bake at 400°F. for 40 minutes or until potatoes are tender. Sprinkle remaining onions over potatoes. Bake 5 minutes more or until onions are golden.   *Serves 4*

CREAMY VEGETABLE MEDLEY

(photo on page 73)

Prep Time: 15 minutes   **Cook Time:** 20 minutes

    1 can (10¾ ounces) CAMPBELL'S Condensed Cream of
         Celery Soup *or* 98% Fat Free Cream of Celery Soup
½ cup milk
    2 cups broccoli flowerets
    2 medium carrots, sliced (about 1 cup)
    1 cup cauliflower flowerets

1 In medium saucepan mix soup, milk, broccoli, carrots and cauliflower. Over medium heat, heat to a boil.

2 Reduce heat to low. Cover and cook 15 minutes or until vegetables are tender, stirring occasionally.   *Serves 6*

Slow Cooker Creations

GOLDEN MUSHROOM PORK & APPLES

Prep Time: 10 minutes   **Cook Time:** 8 to 9 hours

2 cans (10¾ ounces *each*) CAMPBELL'S Condensed Golden Mushroom Soup
½ cup water
1 tablespoon brown sugar
1 tablespoon Worcestershire sauce
1 teaspoon dried thyme leaves, crushed
4 large Granny Smith apples, sliced (about 4 cups)
2 large onions, sliced (about 2 cups)
8 boneless pork chops, ¾ inch thick (about 2 pounds)

In slow cooker mix soup, water, brown sugar, Worcestershire and thyme. Add apples, onions and pork. Cover and cook on **low** 8 to 9 hours or until pork is tender.   *Serves 8*

Top to bottom: Savory Pot Roast (page 89) and Golden Mushroom Pork & Apples

LEMON CHICKEN

Prep Time: 5 minutes   **Cook Time:** 7 to 8 hours

    2 cans (10¾ ounces *each*) CAMPBELL'S Condensed Cream
        of Chicken Soup *or* 98% Fat Free Cream of Chicken
        Soup
    ½ cup water
    ¼ cup lemon juice
    2 teaspoons Dijon-style mustard
    1½ teaspoons garlic powder
    8 large carrots, thickly sliced (about 6 cups)
    8 skinless, boneless chicken breast halves (about
        2 pounds)
    8 cups hot cooked egg noodles
        Grated Parmesan cheese

1 In slow cooker mix soup, water, lemon juice, mustard, garlic
powder and carrots. Add chicken and turn to coat. Cover and
cook on **low** 7 to 8 hours or until chicken is done.

2 Serve over noodles. Sprinkle with cheese.   *Serves 8*

**Top to bottom: Asian Tomato Beef (page 88)
and Lemon Chicken**

ASIAN TOMATO BEEF

(photo on page 87)

Prep Time: 10 minutes   **Cook Time:** 7 to 8 hours and 15 minutes

2 cans (10¾ ounces *each*) CAMPBELL'S Condensed Tomato Soup
⅓ cup soy sauce
⅓ cup vinegar
1½ teaspoons garlic powder
¼ teaspoon pepper
1 (3- to 3½-pound) boneless beef round steak, ¾ inch thick, cut into strips
6 cups broccoli flowerets
8 cups hot cooked rice

1 In slow cooker mix soup, soy sauce, vinegar, garlic powder, pepper and beef. Cover and cook on *low* 7 to 8 hours or until beef is done.

2 Stir. Arrange broccoli over beef. Cover and cook on **high** 15 minutes more or until tender-crisp. Serve over rice.

Serves 8

Tip *No time to chop fresh produce? Buy bags of precut vegetables—they work great in many recipes!*

SAVORY POT ROAST

(photo on page 85)

Prep Time: 10 minutes   **Cook Time:** 8 to 9 hours

    1 can (10¾ ounces) CAMPBELL'S Condensed Cream of
        Mushroom Soup *or* 98% Fat Free Cream of
        Mushroom Soup
    1 pouch CAMPBELL'S Dry Onion Soup and Recipe Mix
    6 medium potatoes, cut into 1-inch pieces (about 6 cups)
    6 medium carrots, thickly sliced (about 3 cups)
    1 (3½- to 4-pound) boneless chuck pot roast, trimmed

In slow cooker mix soup, soup mix, potatoes and carrots. Add roast and turn to coat. Cover and cook on **low** 8 to 9 hours or until roast and vegetables are done.   *Serves 7 to 8*

CREAMY CHICKEN & WILD RICE

(photo on page 91)

Prep Time: 5 minutes   **Cook Time:** 7 to 8 hours

    2 cans (10¾ ounces *each*) CAMPBELL'S Condensed
        Cream of Chicken Soup *or* 98% Fat Free Cream of
        Chicken Soup
 1½ cups water
    1 package (6 ounces) seasoned long-grain and wild
        rice mix
    4 large carrots, thickly sliced (about 3 cups)
    8 skinless, boneless chicken breast halves (about
        2 pounds)

In slow cooker mix soup, water, rice and carrots. Add chicken and turn to coat. Cover and cook on **low** 7 to 8 hours or until chicken and rice are done.   *Serves 8*

NACHO CHICKEN & RICE WRAPS

Prep Time: 5 minutes   **Cook Time:** 7 to 8 hours

2 cans (10¾ ounces *each*) CAMPBELL'S Condensed
Cheddar Cheese Soup
1 cup water
2 cups PACE Thick & Chunky Salsa *or* Picante Sauce
1¼ cups *uncooked* regular long-grain white rice
2 pounds skinless, boneless chicken breasts, cut into
cubes
10 flour tortillas (10-inch)

1 In slow cooker mix soup, water, salsa, rice and chicken. Cover
and cook on **low** 7 to 8 hours or until chicken and rice are
done.

2 Spoon *about 1 cup* rice mixture down center of each tortilla.

3 Fold opposite sides of tortilla over filling. Roll up from bottom.
Cut each wrap in half.   *Serves 10*

Tip   *For firmer rice, substitute converted rice for regular.*

For information on purchasing the *Campbell's* Slow Cooker, please call
1-888-768-7766.

**Top to bottom: Creamy Chicken & Wild Rice (page 89)
and Nacho Chicken & Rice Wrap**

Recipe Index

Product Index